Reluctant journey ...

A pilgrimage of faith from homophobia to Christian love

George S. E. Hopper

Reluctant journey

A pilgrimage of faith from homophobia to Christian love

George S. E. Hopper

Published by the author September 1997
Reprinted November 1997, June 1999, October 2000, March 2003 (with minor amendments)

Editing, design and layout: Andrew Shackleton, Asgard Publishing Services

Printed and bound in Great Britain by
University Print Services. A division of Media Services at Leeds University

ISBN 0 9531168 0 8

British Library Cataloguing in Publication Data
A catalogue record for this book is available from the British Library.

Further copies can be obtained from:

- some bookshops
- EFLGC, 13 Westbrook Drive, Macclesfield, Cheshire SK10 3AQ
  (cheques and postal orders payable to EFLGC)
- LGCM, Oxford House, Derbyshire Street, London E2 6HG
  (cheques and postal orders payable to LGCM)
- the author at: PO Box 5846, Basildon SS15 4GS
  (cheques and postal orders payable to George S. E. Hopper)

Price (including postage & packing):
UK £3.50; Europe £4.20; USA/Middle East £4.75; Australia/Far East £5.00

Text available on the Web at http://www.reluctantjourney.co.uk

Contents

Dedication

I dedicate this simple volume to the following people:

- to my wife, Carol, who accompanied me on this journey of faith;
- to my lesbian and gay Christian friends, in particular those of the Essex Group of the Lesbian and Gay Christian Movement;
- to those Christian friends, including several members of the Church Council from the church where we worship, who with open minds and hearts have listened, thought and prayed, then shared with our lesbian and gay friends;
- to the many people who have contributed to my thinking through the written and spoken word;
- not least to Dougie, the gay man who was courageous enough to come and share something of his life with our Methodist circuit study group, and whose contribution was so vital in helping us to further our understanding;
- finally, and most of all, to our Lord, who called and patiently led me through fear and apprehension to a ministry of love and support for a group of people who are often, like him, despised and rejected.

This book is written in the hope that what I have learned may help towards to the day when fear, ignorance and incorrect assumptions will no longer influence the Church to keep many lesbian and gay Christians at arm's length. They have much to give, and much that they desire to give, and are deeply hurt at the rejection they so often suffer.

As you read, pray! Pray with compassion that God will help you stand in their shoes as Christ stood in ours — to sense what it means to be homosexual, and how much this simple difference affects their lives. Pray that you will read your Bible with an open mind and heart on this matter, and allow the Lord of love and truth to lead you, if necessary, to think what may be for you the unthinkable — the new truth God wants to give you, as he did to Peter in Acts 10.

May God bless you on your pilgrimage of faith, as he has blessed me on mine!

George Hopper

Chapter 1

How this book came to be written

This is no academic treatise, although it is written by a retired scientist/engineer. I have written this book from my own experience. It describes a pilgrimage of faith that began as a challenge to my assumptions about an oppressed group of people. And at its heart is a prayerfully conducted, Christ-centred Bible study. It is a pilgrimage I want to share with you.

Where am I coming from?

My first credential is that I am a Christian from the evangelical wing of the Church who knows his Lord for himself and the power of the Gospel to change and redirect lives. In my case this came about through a 'Damascus Road' conversion that I experienced over 40 years ago. For my wife Carol it took the form of a steady awakening by the Holy Spirit — no less powerful as an instrument of change.

Yet my conversion was no one-off experience. In 1977 our marriage was under considerable strain. While we never ceased to love one another, there was a long period of growing unhappiness and tension caused by pressures of study, work and family that all but destroyed it. Faith hung on a slender thread, after years of prayer that in our distress seemed to have remained unanswered.

Then in one evening a word from the Lord more than restored all that had seemed lost — and in that renewed faith, our marriage has become a rock of 40 years.

These were two of the three most powerful spiritual interventions I have experienced. The third was the awakening that resulted in the pilgrimage of faith described in this book.

My second credential is that I have no personal axe to grind other than the claims of love and justice. I have no homosexual leanings — I'm 100% heterosexual.

Indeed, for most of my life the very thought of what I saw as homosexuality repulsed me. It is no exaggeration to say that I felt physically sick at the thought of what I assumed it to be. And while I would have done nothing to harm homosexuals, I wanted nothing to do with a group of people whom I saw as choosing a way of life that was both unnatural and an offence to God.

Ignorance and biblical literalism had done their dreadful work. Yet these long-held assumptions were soon to be questioned, in a process that began about eight years ago.

Into new truths

The first promptings arose from printed material and responsible television programmes that documented the experience of some homosexual people.

Young people on television spoke of how they had come to realise — sometimes with fear bordering on horror — that they were different from their peers: they were gay. Some of them spoke about the pain they had experienced upon telling their parents, who often found it hard to understand and were sometimes unsupportive. Some young people had even been thrown out of their family home.

Others had grown up within a church community, only to discover that they belonged to the very group that is condemned and rejected by many church people for something over which they (and we) have no control — our sexual orientation.

Another programme included comments from a priest who ministered to people with AIDS and their partners. He said, 'I've learned more about the love of God among these people …'

The result of these and other things I saw, heard and read was that I began to question my assumptions about homosexuality, which I had always thought of as an obsessive sexual perversion, chosen and practised by those involved.

For some time, however, I did no more than think about all this. I made a mental note of such information as came my way, but did little about it. I needed time to assimilate and make sense of these new and unexpected discoveries.

There were other developments that prompted me to rethink my position. About this time, I was preparing to be a local preacher in the Methodist Church. I've always studied the Bible, but I was beginning to learn a great deal more, including the importance of studying the background to the scriptures and how this can help in our understanding and interpretation. I read widely, and my mind was opened to new vistas.

Methodist sexuality report

The next link in the chain was a major report published by the Methodist Church on the subject of human sexuality and its context within the Methodist Church.

I willingly volunteered to join a study group convened by the local Methodist circuit to consider this report. Our deliberations were to take some 18 months to complete.

At one stage we reached a point where we could go no further until we had found answers to some key questions. As a result we heard the evidence of a brave gay man who was prepared to speak openly to us about his life.

This man was unlike the stereotype of the homosexual that I had held in my mind for many years. He asked us not to let go of our Christian compassion in dealing with the issue, and said something that for me was particularly significant: 'Do you think I would choose to be homosexual with all the pain and heartache that goes with it?'

He was the first of many to use such words in my hearing. His experience of life as a homosexual had been painful; he was still mourning the loss of his partner, with whom he had shared his life for over 20 years. He made it clear that, so far as he was concerned, his sexuality was given, not chosen.

The Lord was now speaking clearly and strongly to my mind and heart. One of the crucial issues for me was whether the sexuality of homosexual people was a 'given'. It sounded very much as though it was, and if this were so, then God was there in some way that I and many others had not yet recognised.

Rethinking and re-assessment

I now realised that I would have to begin a complete reappraisal of my thinking and attitudes. But to do this there were two important things that I needed to do:

- I had to obtain more information: reliable information. I was hungry to read what little I could find to enable me to study this issue in the Bible with more understanding.
- I would have to undertake a careful re-examination of the scriptures, in order to see what the Bible really said to me about all this.

I read the Bible through in its entirety for specific reference and context, then began the process of prayerful study and reflection.

When this was finished, I realised I had been wrong. I felt angry with myself for my past attitude, and with those who had reinforced my attitude. I sought God's forgiveness and determined to do what little I could to rectify matters.

Meeting lesbian and gay Christians

Once I had reached this stage in my thinking, I also realised that I needed to meet homosexual Christians and hear their stories. I approached the

Lesbian and Gay Christian Movement (LGCM) and was directed towards the Essex LGCM Group.

This is a group of people who meet for mutual support, prayer, worship, Bible study, communion and various evenings of entertainment together — for example, meals out, visits and car rallies. I have learned a great deal from them, and have met many fine Christian people among them.

Since that time my wife Carol and I continued to meet with lesbian and gay Christians, for worship, fellowship and social get-togethers. They came to our home; we went to theirs. We learned to love them with the love of Christ.

They welcomed us — representatives of those who have hurt them — into their support group. I find their faith amazing. To hold to Christ when many (though not all) find the Church is spiteful to them, shows a true faith.

I have seen enough and shared enough with these people to want to see them affirmed and loved in the Church — able to enter fully into the life of the Church at every level. **When I am with these friends, I feel close to Christ!** Perhaps this is because they, like him, know what it is to be despised and rejected, and yet show patient love and understanding in return.

Searching the scriptures

My third credential is that I am a keen Bible student — I wear Bibles out!

And there are some important things that I have learned about the Bible. It may be published in impeccable English and bound within beautifully designed modern covers — often leading people to think it is modern — but it certainly cannot be read as a modern book.

Neither is it a textbook on religious laws! It is an ancient book — one which contains the way of salvation. And on many subjects it is like a deep gold mine, for the most part requiring open heart and mind, hard work and prayer to mine the true gold, especially when dealing with complex issues like the one in question here.

Certainly there are verses that are readily understood, and that can become to us the Word of God in our need, as Isaiah 26:3 became for Carol and me one January night in 1977 and saved our marriage. But for the most part the Bible requires patient study, an understanding of the people who wrote the words, their times and culture, the context in which they were writing, and not least an understanding of the issue we are examining. **For incorrect assumptions lead to false conclusions!**

And finally, I knew that the issue must be considered in the context of the *whole* Bible, with Jesus, the Living Word, as the final arbiter. To study the Bible superficially — to look up a series of references and think that we have the 'Bible view' on an issue — is, sadly, often to abuse the Word of God.

So as we go on to study the Bible in relation to homosexuality, and in particular to homosexual Christians, we shall follow the same study and thought processes that the Lord has led me through. We shall consider *all* the references in the context (as far as possible) of the culture and times in which they were written, and with objective knowledge of the issue.

New truth, new leading

The next point may be reassuring for those of you who find the whole issue of homosexuality very threatening. For in those early days, as I turned prayerfully to the Bible for guidance, prepared to let the Holy Spirit lead me, I began to feel not a little threatened by the new truth into which my Lord was leading me. It was shaking some of my foundations — I know how Peter felt in Acts 10 as the Lord began to show him new truths about what is clean and unclean. I prayed earnestly that I would not be misled one way or another. I did not want to dishonour my Lord and my God; that is the spirit in which this whole biblical pilgrimage has been conducted.

As I proceeded and the way become clearer, I experienced that well-known sinking feeling: if the Lord showed me what I thought he was about to show me, he would also expect me to meet and share with, and perhaps even identify with, his lesbian and gay Christian followers — just as he had with me!

Well, he did show me what I had expected, and he did expect me to act just as I thought he would. But this no longer feels threatening now. It is something I do gladly in fellowship with these precious new-found Christian friends of mine.

It was difficult at first, but with my new understanding I have done what little I can in the church where I worship. I have led discussions and Bible studies on the issue. And eventually, with the help of John, the Convenor of the Essex LGCM Group, Carol and I have brought some of our heterosexual and homosexual Christian friends together in a social atmosphere in an endeavour to help others move towards a similar understanding.

In a much more limited way, I have occasionally raised the subject within appropriate contexts in talks and sermons. The response to this has, for the most part, been positive. I have also corresponded with some who have not been led to the same conclusions as I have. On one occasion I responded more fully to a Baptist minister I had gone to hear, and who had spoken courageously to his congregation on the issue, but whose insufficiency of knowledge had led to conclusions that were questionable.

It was in carrying out this last task that the Lord led me to set about writing down my experiences and making the account into a book.

Why am I doing all this?

1. Out of Christian love

I recognise the problems people have in understanding when they have no real opportunity, as I have had, to study, research, and talk and listen to gay and lesbian Christians. And I am writing out of Christian love for these, my gay and lesbian Christian friends — for we are one in Christ Jesus.

2. Out of a passion for justice

I hate injustice of any kind, and long for reconciliation. The people who are the subject of this book have been badly mistreated in the world — by society and by the Church. Many thousands of gay men were victims of the Holocaust along with Jews and others thought by the Nazis to be inferior.

And many of us today simply ostracise homosexual men or women, even those who are Christians, refusing to recognise them, and trying to find theories as to why they are as they are so we can 'heal' them, 'convert' them — anything but accept them and love them in Christ.

It is time for the Church to say 'No' to this attitude, and to welcome such Christians as the loving, faithful people they are.

3. Out of a vision of reconciliation

These are momentous times. Who would have thought the Berlin Wall would ever come down, or apartheid be abandoned, or women welcomed into the ministry and priesthood, or peace become even a possibility in Northern Ireland? God is at work in all sorts of ways, tearing down barriers, just as he did at Calvary.

The barriers that have kept his beloved gay and lesbian people from full recognition and ministry also need sweeping away.

If this small volume helps towards love, justice and reconciliation — if I can play a small part in this process — I will be very glad.

Chapter 2

What is homosexuality and how does it come about?

It is in people's assumptions about the nature of homosexuality that much of the misunderstanding lies, leading many to draw faulty conclusions as to what God's will is for gay and lesbian people, especially those who are Christian. First we need to be clear about the term 'homosexuality', because it is so often used loosely — as a kind of 'catch-all' that not only reveals confusion in the minds of those using it, but also perpetuates that confusion.

Many who oppose homosexuality in the Church think they know what this is all about, and rush to express opinions about those affected. I recognise these opinions — they were once my own. But I have yet to hear anyone who is critical about homosexuality express a correct understanding of the matter.

We regularly hear phrases such as 'sexual preferences', 'choosing their way', 'sexuality caused by bad parent–child relationships' etc. — sometimes from people who should know better. They clearly have neither weighed the evidence available, nor listened to the people they so freely discuss. Perhaps they are afraid to hear or accept new truths, or think that the evidence offered by homosexual people is tainted — or, perhaps worst of all, they have closed their minds, treating the Bible as a textbook of religious laws, thinking that the Holy Spirit has given them an interpretation that can't be challenged.

Since I've learned more on the subject myself, I have found that most of what we hear in conversations or sermons, and read in newspapers, is misleading. 'Homosexual' is *not* another word for 'paedophile'; children are as safe with gay men as with heterosexual men. There are abusers among them, just as there are those who are sexually obsessed or perverted, but they are no more prevalent than among heterosexuals. Equally, there are many fine, gifted, faithful people among them, just as there are among heterosexuals. Homosexuals rarely fit the stereotypes of butch females and effeminate men, which is why they are usually unrecognised in churches and society until they 'come out'. Certainly, those whom I know are just ordinary people living ordinary lives like you and me.

Nevertheless, while there is obviously much misinformation, there are well-informed, responsible TV programmes and research writings. I have also found that lesbian and gay people are often very willing to speak of their experiences to people they trust, and their accounts are invaluable to us in learning about the issues.

What is homosexuality?

Let's start at the beginning, always bearing in mind that if we turn to the scriptures without a good knowledge of the issue we are studying, we will mislead ourselves by misinterpreting, and therefore dishonouring, the Word of God.

The answer to this first question is straightforward. The *only* difference between those of us who are heterosexual and those who are homosexual is in the nature of our natural sexual attraction. Most of us are heterosexual, possessing a natural sexual attraction for the opposite sex. Homosexual people are by nature sexually attracted to the same sex. This is their natural sexual affection — no less natural than the heterosexual attraction towards the opposite sex.

However, the word 'homosexual' is loosely used to include different groups of people, and this can lead to considerable confusion.

True homosexuals are people with a natural sexual attraction to others of the same sex. No amount of prayer, counselling, Christian healing or deliverance can change their sexuality. They are homosexual by nature (we shall consider what this means later). They express their sexuality in ways similar to those practised by heterosexuals, though as with heterosexuals this expression might take many different forms such as celibacy, 'courting' or more intimate expression.

Just like the rest of us, homosexuals include many who are responsible, faithful and truly loving in the way they express their sexuality towards the person they love. (This is how I find those of my homosexual Christian friends who are in covenant relationships.) There are also homosexuals (*and* heterosexuals) who express their sexuality in exploitative and damaging ways, destroying their own dignity and that of others.

Then there are **same-sex sexual adventurers** — not bisexual people (see below) but heterosexuals who engage in same-sex acts for various reasons: money, experimentation, sexual obsession or, in the case of men, lack of female opportunity. This used to be found mainly in single-sex institutions, prisons, armed forces etc. but is now reported to be much more widespread in a 'sexually freer' society. It is these people that need healing to be restored to their true sexuality.

Finally, to add to the confusion, there are **bisexual people**, who are sexually attracted to people of both sexes. It has been suggested that human sexuality is on a continuum, with 100% heterosexuality at one extreme, 100% homosexuality at the other and bisexuality in between. This fits the experience of many people.

It is easy to see how confusion can occur when the term 'homosexuality' is used without qualification. There is a variety about all aspects of God's creation, some of which stuns us with its beauty and some of which requires our understanding and compassion.

For the purposes of this study, I wish to confine myself to true homosexuals — people who are sexually attracted to those of the same sex and who, because it is part of their given nature, cannot be changed. **And for the most part I wish to speak with reference to homosexual Christians, and others who are responsible in expressing their sexuality.**

Once we have reached the end of this study, the place of bisexual people in the love of God will, I hope, become a little clearer.

Is homosexuality a 'given'?

What evidence is there that homosexual orientation is a given state?

There is much compelling evidence, most of it relating to men, though it has to be said that some of the evidence, while pointing in a particular direction, is not finally conclusive. But taken together with the evidence of the experience of gay and lesbian people themselves, it does points to their sexuality being a 'given'.

So let's look at the evidence, but only after dispelling one false assumption that is the root of misunderstanding for some. Most people know that our X and Y chromosome patterns, with a very few exceptions (see page 16), determine our physical gender attributes (i.e. whether we have the bodies of men or of women). What is not so well understood is that the processes that determine our physical gender do not also determine our sexuality. Other processes determine this.

Essentially, there are three principal theories about how our sexuality is determined: the **nurture** theory, the **choice** theory and **nature** theory.

Nurture

The first theory — unlikely from the evidence available — is that sexuality is governed by early child–parent relationships. In the case of boys, the theory states that the father–son relationship is very important to the right development of the son's sexuality; a bad father–son relationship, or the absence of the father, may lead to an over-close mother–son relationship that in turn predisposes the son towards homosexuality.

Some supporting this theory fear that the present high rate of family break-up and divorce will lead to an unusually high number of gay men. Yet one doesn't have to look far to discover that the theory is highly questionable and does not fit the facts.

For instance, were there unusually large, even vast numbers of gay men as a result of the war years taking fathers away? And what of the many children raised in families where damaged relationships seem almost to be the norm?

The evidence from gay people themselves is that, like the rest of us, some had poor childhood relationships with dad, some with mum, and many had a happy childhood.

If this theory had any credence, it would enable the proponents to find and offer effective methods of healing. Yet the evidence of successful healing is signally lacking, as many true gay men have found who have wanted to be the same as other people. Their difference causes them much pain in our society in the various ways they are oppressed. Suffice it to say that many lesbian and gay people laugh in frustration at this theory — and with good reason, as you will see.

Choice

The second theory is that gay and lesbian people choose their sexuality.

I have only to ask you this question: did you choose your sexuality? Of course you did not. Sexuality is an integral part of all of us, however it has developed.

Yet the choice theory and the nurture theory, in various mixed measures, are the basic foundation underlying the viewpoint of many who seek to offer 'Christian help' to homosexual people to 'repent' of their homosexuality. The help they are offering is undoubtedly well-meant, but it is based on a misunderstanding of homosexuality and a misinterpretation of the scriptures, and is therefore misguided. Such 'help' can cause real distress.

The only healing needed is the affirmation and love that Christ offers — and forgiveness for any who have strayed into abuse of their sexuality.

How we *express* our sexuality is something we *do* choose — whether to enrich another's life as well as our own, or to use it in ways that destroy our own dignity and that of others. But that's another thing entirely.

One opinion commonly expressed by Christian homosexuals is particularly telling: 'Do you think I would choose to be homosexual, with all the pain that goes with it, if I had the choice?'

Among the Christian gay people I have met are some who at one stage have tried everything they could to be rid of their homosexual feelings — years of praying; counselling from Christians and others; Christian healing and deliverance ministry; therapy from professionals — all to no avail.

One such person that I didn't meet, but whose story is well known, was Simon Harvey — a young Christian who did everything he could possibly do to be rid of his homosexual feelings, but without success. He was desperate to change, and his despair led to suicide.

Others have followed the advice given by well-meaning but misinformed counsellors that they should marry to rid themselves of their homosexual feelings. Most such marriages are a recipe for disaster.

There is no way for true homosexuals to change their sexuality, though some in the Church do offer ways, and in the name of God cause some homosexual people much emotional damage. Depression, even suicidal thinking, can be the negative results of such attempted 'healings' that undermine the given personality of true homosexual people.

Throughout history, gay men in particular have been persecuted in the most terrible ways — thrown into asylums, tortured, put to death. And today, they are blackmailed, beaten up, murdered, rejected in various ways — some subtle, some not so subtle. They have no prospect of children and family in the accepted sense — something which causes many to feel a great sense of loss.

Given all these pressures upon homosexual people, we can be sure that most of them — Christians especially — would indeed have changed their sexuality if they could possibly have done so.

They are denied a rightful place in God's kingdom — not by God in Jesus, but by many who call themselves his people — although we can thank God that, under the guidance of his Holy Spirit, more and more of his people are coming to see their ignorance and repent of their attitudes, just as I have.

Thankfully, the climate is slowly changing. There are now support groups, helplines and other ways of helping those who find they are homosexual to realise that, while they may be different from many others, they are a very significant group in society and their sexuality is quite normal for them — nothing to be ashamed of but rather to thank God for and rejoice in.

Many are helped through these support agencies to find and accept themselves as they are — though it is still hard even for these, the more fortunate ones, because of the prejudice and ignorance that is still rife.

Sadly, there are many who just cannot face the consequences openly — lives blighted by pious bigotry, ignorance and prejudice. I sometimes wonder, how angry does this make God?

Nature

The third theory is that our sexuality is a given part of our nature, whether we are heterosexual or homosexual — and there is a lot of evidence that supports this. Here are some examples of such evidence:

1. The experience of gay and lesbian people is that their sexuality is a 'given' part of their make-up. Their only choice, like everyone else's, is how they are to express it.

2. Powerful aversion therapy has been used to try to 'cure' homosexuals of their sexuality. Such methods have proved successful with 'learned behaviour' in the sexual sphere such as fetishes, but unsuccessful when used to 'cure' homosexuals of their sexuality. This would suggest that homosexuality is not something that is 'learned'.

3. A Dominican family that has been the subject of much research has, over a period of about 140 years, produced among the many children nearly 40 who were girls at birth and were raised as girls, but who at puberty become young men with no serious effects on their male sexuality. This is evidence that certainly refutes the 'nurture' theory.

4. An East German scientist followed up some research into the behaviour of lower mammals which showed that interfering with testosterone flow during critical stages in foetal development produced homosexual behaviour in the resulting male offspring. Postulating from this that the brains of homosexual male mammals had been somehow 'feminised', he carried out experiments that supported his hypothesis. He then repeated the tests on two groups of men: a homosexual group and a heterosexual group. He found that when oestrogen was introduced into the bodies of homosexual men, this produced an ovulating hormone response (even though there were no ovaries present), whereas there was no such response in the heterosexual men. This would suggest that there are hidden but significant differences between homosexual and heterosexual men. I should add that this work has been challenged.

5. Other work being carried out by scientists with male homosexuals in the United States, including twin studies, suggests increasingly that the two major factors that determine sexuality are genetic make-up and foetal development in the womb. But the work is not yet complete.

6. Among various mammal and bird populations there is a significant proportion of animals that exhibit homosexual behaviour. Homosexuality, it would appear, is a natural part of animal behaviour as a whole.

We can conclude from all this that most of the evidence, while not definitive, strongly suggests that sexual orientation is a matter of nature, rather than of nurture or choice, neither of which has much real evidence to support it. Furthermore, if sexual orientation is a matter of nature, then we are dealing here with something that is a 'given'.

If our sexuality is a 'given', then it is a gift from God

There have always been homosexual people; they are a natural part of the human population. Homosexuality is a natural, healthy sexuality in its loving expression, just as is heterosexuality. To compare homosexuals, as some do, with those who sexually abuse others (e.g. paedophiles) reveals deep ignorance and does grave damage.

The problem lies not in being gay or lesbian, but in living in an ignorant, fearful, condemnatory, rejecting world. Homosexual people are diminished and their dignity undermined when they are not acknowledged or affirmed as heterosexual people are. They cannot be fully themselves when part of their nature is denied.

In spite of all the pressures, however — and I find this astonishing — homosexual relationships can be as loving, committed, long-term, faithful and happy as any heterosexual relationship, including marriage. I have seen this, and seen the grief when a long-term partner has died. Other Christians have also told me of gay relationships that 'if all marriages were as happy, the world would be a better place.'

Yet the pain of being homosexual in a heterosexual world is real. To help you appreciate this, I've written the next chapter, **Standing in their shoes**, in the form of a little story. Please enter into the spirit of it.

Chapter 3

Standing in their shoes

I ask you now to use your imagination and to read this carefully, perhaps more than once. For this is your chance to 'feel' what the world is like for homosexual people.

An exercise in imagination

For just a few moments I want you to imagine yourself in a world in which

- You are a lonely heterosexual in a homosexual world.
- Only homosexual unions can produce children.
- Society and the Church both declare in their different ways that your heterosexuality is perverse and evil.
- The scriptures are essentially homosexual in culture, and are interpreted as stating that heterosexuals and heterosexuality are wicked, though Jesus, the Lord, the Living Word and inspiration of the Church, has nothing to say on this in the Gospels. You wonder why, if Jesus said nothing, the Church does not act in the spirit of Christ — the spirit of Christian compassion and love.
- Platonic friendship between the sexes is the norm and is encouraged. But potential meeting places are all for both sexes to ensure that people of the same sex are not alone together.

Into such a world you are born and grow up in a devout, committed Christian family. As a schoolboy you had a crush on a woman teacher, but this is considered quite normal. (From now on, women readers may wish to switch 'male' for 'female' and visa versa.)

As a young male teenager you are disturbed to find that you feel a strange attraction to girls when all your male friends are dating boys.

One girl in particular is very difficult to put out of your mind, but you know this is unnatural and try very hard not to think of her. Yet as you continue to grow, so (to your dismay) do the feelings of attraction towards the opposite sex. You wonder what is the matter with you — you feel disgusted with yourself.

To compound this, the preacher's topic at church is sexual sin. He speaks quietly but firmly of the evils of heterosexuality, saying that heterosexuals cannot be Christian. He preaches that such people choose to encourage their heterosexual feelings. You feel despair!

You have already responded to Christ and live your life as a disciple. You read the Bible devoutly, and Jesus' teaching influences what you are and do. You give generously of what God has given you and you receive the sacraments which mean much to you. For love of Christ and the world which he and you love, you are deeply involved in serving others.

Can these feelings stand between you and your Lord? They have not affected any other aspect of your discipleship. But can you be heterosexual *and* Christian? The preacher seemed to think not.

You speak to your minister, and he warns you of your feelings, which if not dealt with may destroy your life and faith. He suggests you find a fine young man to marry, and get rid of your heterosexual feelings. You take his advice, and throw yourself into a relationship, then marriage, with a man you much admire. Your friends are overjoyed; they previously wondered if you would ever marry, because you've never had boyfriends before.

Then one day you are out with a female friend shopping. As you talk, you find her warm and understanding. As friends, you confide in each other about the past. And as you talk, your heart sinks — there is the old stirring inside you. You try not to think of her, or see her. But when you do see her your emotions go haywire, and it becomes increasingly obvious she feels something very special for you. But it must remain secret; you can share your joy with nobody.

The sheer delight of loving her (for it is love) is accompanied by disgust and self-loathing. You pray to God as you have never prayed before to change you. You go back to your minister and share your distress. He tells you of people who can help you — people who have healed heterosexuals in the power of God. You keep praying for deliverance; this threatens your whole life! You go to all those who claim to be able to help. But they only leave you in a state of despair. For nothing has changed except your feelings of guilt and desperation, which have merely grown stronger.

You wonder if you should simply end it all. You just cannot continue in a state of deception, yet you must in order to keep your marriage and your place in the church. What a mess you feel — torn apart! Your love for Christ; your love for your female friend, which can never be recognised and which is condemned as unnatural, yet is so natural to you; your marriage, which is now making you and your partner unhappy. The last thing you want is to hurt him, because you care for him deeply, though you have never felt what you feel for your female friend. What are you to do?

You know of some like you who have decided to stop the pretence, and have quietly let it be known who they really are. Some of these have experienced the trauma of attacks — verbal and sometimes physical. Many of those who are Christians have been eased or pushed out of the Church. Some, more fortunate, have been understood and loved. Yet you know of others who have tried to keep their secret to themselves only to be blackmailed by nasty, greedy people who have guessed their secret.

What would be the response if you took the courageous step of being honest with your fellow-Christians?

How does that feel?

The scenario I have asked you to imagine is just one unending story from among many possible stories that illustrate the pain experienced by people who are different, and whom we try hard to pressure into our conformity.

How did you feel standing in their shoes?

Some real-life stories

I could tell you several true stories about gay men.

There was one man who frequented the 'gay scene', where he could meet people of like sexuality and feel relaxed for a while, knowing he was in the company of those who understood him, but equally where there were temptations to which he yielded. Coming home, tired and disgusted with himself, he cried out to God to help him. And there on the London bus alone, he met with his loving Creator God. His life was changed: he learned to pray, to allow Christ through the scriptures to influence his life. But his sexuality was still the same, although now he lived for Christ. He felt it was time to find a church to share in the worship of the God who had called and blessed him. But this is when his problems began!

'It would be better if you went elsewhere' was the rejoinder when he finally told his story to his pastor because when preparing for baptism he thought he should share who he was and remove any deceit.

I could also tell you about a fine Christian man who found Christ in an evangelistic crusade. He too left the gay scene, and his partner — for he was assured that Christianity and his gay partnership were inconsistent, even when based on Christian love for one another. But his gay feelings have never changed, even though he has sought help from those offering it through the Church — counselling; exorcism; prayer.

He is a man of high integrity, and one of the most faithful Christians it has been my privilege to meet; who has struggled to reconcile his faith with his sexuality. He still has no partner, but knows that like others he needs love. Thankfully, he now recognises that God loves him with his sexuality as it is — and with a partner, too, if God should send along 'Mr Right'.

The church that he loved, and where he wished to serve, has now eased him out. So it is not surprising that he is losing faith with the Church, though thankfully not with Christ.

I shall now talk about a woman for a change, and tell a story that, unusually, has better ending. She has always been involved in the Church, and a very gifted woman she is too. She has gone through life without any loves, until she recently met her partner.

As she describes it, 'I felt abhorrence like everybody else about homosexuality, though it never entered my life in any way. I didn't think much about it. Then one day I found this was me!'

She and her partner, both Christian women, are among the more fortunate. They both love Christ and the Church, and while they were unable to get permission for blessing on their union in church, they were allowed to receive a blessing in their home. Perhaps such women are seen as less of a threat, somehow.

If only people realised there are homosexual men and women all round them. They are ordinary people, and no threat to them except possibly to their attitudes.

Carol and I count among our many friends certain ministers, lay readers and preachers, choristers, organists and church members — all fine Christian people, and all of them homosexual.

Having discussed who the people are that we are talking about, let us now go on to look at the kinds of tools we need in order to make proper sense of what the scriptures really say about homosexuality.

Chapter 4

Bibles and Bible study

The first question we need to ask is which Bible to use. For there are many different translations of the Bible. Most of us are not Hebrew or Greek scholars, so we rely on biblical translators to do this work faithfully for us. Can we rely on them? It may come as a surprise to discover that Bible versions differ, and that some are not suited to serious study.

Translators and editors have different priorities in mind when preparing their own particular version for publication. Some versions are created for ease of reading or for use in worship; others concentrate on accuracy of meaning, with the translators working hard to provide the best approximation to what the original writer was actually saying. Sometimes this is an almost impossible task, and the best study Bibles will explain the specific problem and what the translators think is the most likely meaning.

One thing that I find difficult to understand is that some Bible translations seem to be biased towards a particular theological viewpoint. And sadly, one particular favourite is unintentionally flawed.

How, then, can we find out which versions are reliable for study?

Read the introduction

When considering a particular study Bible, always look carefully at the preface and/or introduction to ensure that it is suitable for serious study. Try to find answers to the following questions:

- Who initiated the particular version under consideration, and for what reason?
- Who were the translators, and what were their backgrounds?
- What was the primary aim? Was it accuracy of translation, readability, or suitability for worship or drama? Is it a paraphrase, for example?
- What methods were employed to obtain the best translation and eliminate bias, whether sectarian or theological?
- Where translation problems occur, how are they handled? Are they indicated by means of footnotes or some other means?

- Is the version supported by internationally respected Bible societies?

Versions used for study

While there are doubtless other suitable Bibles, there are three versions that I personally use for study, having considered them in relation to the criteria given above:

Revised Standard Version (RSV); New Revised Standard Version (NRSV); Good News Bible (GNB)
The GNB is designed to read more easily than the RSV and NRSV, but all three have been created with accuracy of meaning as a major criterion.

All are produced by teams of scholars, working with each other and with other responsible bodies in such a way as to eliminate bias and achieve accuracy of meaning as far as it is possible to do so. They talk honestly about the problems of translation, and provide footnotes where there are difficulties or uncertainties that remain. All three have the imprimatur of the British and Foreign Bible Society.

Nevertheless no version, however reliably translated — and none is totally reliable — can do all our work for us. We need to study widely and think hard to find sound biblical answers to our questions, especially when developing knowledge throws new light on a particular matter, as is the case with the question we are now examining.

Versions used for comparison purposes

There are two other versions of the Bible that I use, mainly just for the purposes of comparison, as their prefaces suggest a particular theological viewpoint:

New International Version (NIV)
The NIV is evangelical in origin, but I have not noticed any particular bias on the issue of homosexuality. This version has the imprimatur of the International Bible Society (formerly the New York Bible Society).

However, I would raise a cautionary point regarding the notes included in the NIV Study Version, as these seem to display an inadequate understanding of the issue in question here.

Jerusalem Bible (JB)
This version is Roman Catholic in origin. Though it has been translated by 27 scholars, the final result is the responsibility of one man: Alexander Jones. It has the imprimatur of the late Cardinal Heenan, former Archbishop of Westminster, and the Study Version notes take account of Vatican 2 decisions.

Some versions unsuitable for critical study

Paraphrases

Paraphrases inevitably reflect the theological views of the writers, and if used, they should be used with the utmost care (the same is true of many, if not most, Bible commentaries).

This applies to the widely used **Living Bible**, which is a paraphrase. It is also written from the rigid conservative evangelical tradition (this is declared in the preface to the early edition, but is sadly omitted in later editions). The Living Bible does not have the imprimatur of any Bible society, and like any paraphrase it should never be used for serious study.

King James Version (KJV)

Finally, what about the much-loved King James or Authorised Version? Sadly, it contains many inaccuracies, and many of the words and phrases no longer mean what they did when it was translated. **It has also been a principal contributor to serious misunderstanding on the issue of homosexuality** — as you will soon discover.

Also, the codices of the scriptures, upon which those early translators based their work honourably and well, are now known to have contained flaws — mistakes made over many centuries by those copying the scriptures from manuscript to manuscript. The overall result is a version that suffers from accumulated errors. It is a salutary exercise to read the preface to the RSV, which explains why it was necessary to replace the King James Version!

I still continue to use this version, among others, for its intrinsic beauty of expression — but never for study.

The tools for Bible study

When studying, make sure you use suitable, reliable versions, with good reference aids where possible.

I personally use the RSV, NRSV and GNB, and for comparison I look at the NIV and JB to see if they add to understanding. An analytical concordance and a Bible dictionary are also very useful tools, as are other reference books on such subjects as culture, beliefs etc. (see also the bibliography at the end).

But above all it is vital that you bring to your study an open, enquiring mind, ready to ask God about what you have found — a mind ready to receive the truth that God wants to give you. Remember, too, that this will only be a small part — perhaps only the beginning — of God's revelation. We never cease learning about our amazing God and his love.

The scriptures were written by God-inspired messengers who wrote in the context of their times, their understanding of the world, their culture. We usually need to know about these to unlock the meaning that the writer is trying to convey. So we have to work hard at obtaining a good general knowledge of the customs, culture, beliefs, times and history in which the scriptures were written. These are vital to our understanding of why things were written as they were. The more we know about these things, the better we will understand the scriptures — they will come alive! — and the more likely we are to discover the 'kernel' of God's word.

Some words of reassurance

Before we embark on this voyage of discovery, I should like to add just a few words of reassurance.

I didn't *just* look up the particular Bible passages that we shall be examining in the chapters that follow. I first read the Bible all the way through (in the RSV translation) in order to gain a balanced view, in the context of the whole, of what it its writers were saying on sexual matters, and especially about sexual sinfulness.

Only then did I begin to concentrate on the references that relate to — or at least appear to relate to — the study, all of which we shall go on to examine.

In this way I tried to make sure as far as possible that I had missed nothing of any significance.

I shall start this biblical journey by giving an overview of what I found, and then go into the detail about the specific references considered by many to relate to homosexuality and to condemn it.

Chapter 5

The Bible — an overview

We can now continue with our Bible study, armed with a few facts that we need to remember:

- The natural affection, or sexual attraction, of true homosexuals is for people of the same sex, and is normally expressed towards other homosexuals. Like heterosexuals, they do not choose their sexuality — it is a given part of their natural make-up and cannot be changed.
- Heterosexuals who engage in same-sex sexual acts (and there are many if surveys are to be believed) **are *not* homosexuals**.

Our purpose is to examine the assertion of those who declare that the Bible clearly and unequivocally condemns homosexuality. For what I found when I read the Bible through with open mind and heart, and with a better knowledge of homosexuality, was something quite different.

It certainly condemns anybody, heterosexual or homosexual, indulging in any kind of sexual behaviour that exploits, abuses and destroys or undermines the dignity of those involved. But does it say anything about the given sexuality that we call homosexuality, and which we now know is simply the sexual orientation given to homosexuals to be attracted towards others of the same sex? And in particular, has it anything to say about the truly loving sexual expression by homosexual people — male and female — within a committed, faithful, stable relationship?

We are going to examine each Bible reference that has been used against homosexuals, but only after we have had a brief overview of key parts of the Bible that are used in order to judge the issue. For it is the contention of those who see condemnation of homosexuality in the Bible that the word is plain and unambiguous. Yet when we look at the homosexuality issue in context, we find that the situation is quite different, at least where homosexual love is expressed in a loving, committed, faithful, stable relationship. Jesus often turned things upside down and he so does in this. It is those who condemn others who find themselves condemned (Matthew 7:1; John 3:16–17).

We now set out on the first part of a fascinating journey! It begins with an interesting, indeed astonishing, observation that I made when I read the Bible through for reference and context on this issue.

I looked at certain key parts of the Bible that contain many of the laws on which great civilisations have been based. I wanted to see if these key sections contained anything on homosexuality:

- Was there anything in Exodus and Deuteronomy, both of which contain the Ten Commandments, the Book of the Covenant, and many other laws?
- Was there anything in the Gospels of Jesus, the Living Word?

If homosexuality (like adultery and prostitution) is the big moral issue in the Bible that some say it is, I certainly expected to find guidance on the issue here in these great books! I noted each reference to sexual sin that was to be found there, and this is what I found:

The Book of Exodus

Exodus 20:1–17
Is there anything among the **Ten Commandments**, the great laws given by God for an orderly, caring society? Not a word — but adultery is mentioned in verse 14, and lust in verse 17.

Exodus 20:22 – 23:33
Is there anything in this the **Book of the Covenant**, which is directly associated with the Ten Commandments? Seduction of a virgin is referred to in 22:16, and bestial sex in 22:19 — otherwise, not a word!

This means there is not a single reference to homosexuality, either directly or indirectly, in Exodus, this great book of the Law!

The Book of Deuteronomy

This book contains a 'copy of the law' (in Greek *to deuteron* means 'the second time', while *ho nomos* means 'the Law'). It does, however, differ in some ways from Exodus.

Deuteronomy 5:6–21
The **Ten Commandments** contain the same strictures on adultery in verse 18 and on lust in verse 21 — but still nothing on homosexuality.

Deuteronomy 12:1 – 26:19
The **Book of the Covenant** is rather longer here than in Exodus. There are references to the sexual sins of adultery, lust, fornication, rape and incest in 22:20–30. Then there is a reference to the male same-sex sin in 23:17, which the King James Version mistranslates thus:

> 'There shall be ... no sodomite of the sons of Israel.'

This and similar references in the Books of Kings are examples of where the King James Version has caused confusion and done considerable damage to the image of homosexuals.

The Hebrew word *qadesh* or 'separated ones', which is translated 'sodomite' in the KJV, actually refers to the male temple prostitutes who were involved in the hated sexual practices associated with fertility cult worship among the people of Canaan.

Reliable modern versions of the Bible correct this error. Take a look for yourself at Deuteronomy 23:17. The NIV, for example, says:

> 'No Israelite … is to become a temple prostitute.'

Deuteronomy 27:11ff
Here we find the blessings and curses delivered by Moses before the Israelites entered the Promised Land. Among the curses, he refers to the sexual sins of incest and bestiality (27:20–23). But there is no mention, here or in any other part of Deuteronomy, of homosexuality expressed in real love.

The Four Gospels

What about the Gospels? Surely Jesus, the Living Word of God, would have something to say if homosexuality were sinful and wicked.

Well, Jesus did have things to say about sexual failure and sin, especially adultery and lust (although he did not take the hard line taken in the Law). But he said no word about homosexuality — nothing whatsoever!

If my experience of homosexual Christians is anything to go by, Jesus would have welcomed them as his friends, just as he has led me to do.

A surprising conclusion

It is surely extremely surprising that in key sections of the Bible containing laws that are the basis of great civilisations — Exodus, Deuteronomy and the Gospels — there is no mention of homosexuality (by which of course we mean the given disposition of gay and lesbian people to be attracted to others of the same sex, and its loving, responsible expression towards the one who is loved).

Let us now proceed to look in more detail at passages where critics state that condemnation of homosexuality is either indicated to or implied.

Chapter 6

Old Testament references

Genesis 13:13; 19:1–11
The story of Sodom and Gomorrah

This story has done more damage to the image and status of homosexuals than perhaps any other part of the Bible. Yet when we read it carefully, we find that we are not told the sexuality of the offenders. What we are told, in Genesis 13:13, is that those involved were 'wicked, great sinners' [NRSV]. The passage aptly describes them. They were guilty of:

- **the intended rape of the guests:** they were both intimidating and violent in their manner; **but if this is a story about intended male rape *per se***, why did they not rape Lot who went out to them?
- **the grossest inhospitality:** in a land where hospitality was of the highest importance (as it still is), and the host was responsible for the safety and well-being of his guests, Lot was more willing to offer his daughters than let his guests be abused.

Interestingly, Jesus referred to this story not in the way that many interpret it, but in the context of **inhospitality** (Matthew 10:11–15; Luke 10:8–12), **unbelief** (Matthew 11:20–24) and **unpreparedness** (Luke 17:28–30).

The issue here is *not* the sexuality of the offenders (which we are not told), but the violent intentions of wicked men wishing to destroy Lot's reputation as a host by abusing his guests.

We can only guess at the reasons — perhaps jealousy at Lot's wealth? Or suspicions about racial or cultural differences, or about the separateness of those people whose God was Yahweh? These are similar to the motives that cause people nowadays to mistreat outsiders or perceived intruders. The homosexuals I know are as horrified at this kind of behaviour as any other responsible person would be.

Doubtless there are wicked men, homosexual or heterosexual, who would do such things, but we don't know the sexuality of those in the story. It can't be important, or we would have been told.

The issue the writer is addressing is the demonstrable wickedness of the people in the story. It is about as far removed as one can get from the enriching, faithful love that responsible homosexuals, especially Christians, can share, and which is the burden of this study. It has absolutely nothing to do with the issue.

There is, however, another possible explanation for this story being included in the Bible. Sodom gave its name to the sexual act that the Israelites normally associated with cult male prostitution (of which more anon). Now cult prostitution was hated by the faithful Israelites. So if the cities of Sodom and Gomorrah were burned when tar pits (now known to exist in that area) were ignited, then cult prostitution may have provided the Israelites with a ready-made explanation of why God should have punished the people of Sodom.

The Israelites always had to find such a reason for people's misfortunes — it was the way they thought, and continued to do so even in Jesus' day (see John 9:1–2 and Luke 13:1–4). This explanation would have served as a suitable warning to any young Israelite who was tempted to get involved in cult prostitution.

Judges 19:16–28

These verses contain an almost identical story to that of Sodom, except that here the culprits were from the tribe of Benjamin, and their actions included violent *heterosexual* rape leading to the death of the guest's concubine (although they initially demanded that the male visitor be given to them). Again, the host went out to them, but they wanted the guest. Their punishment was a war that decimated the tribe (Judges 20).

Much the same comment applies as to the story in Genesis. The sexuality of the offenders is not given. The issue is gross inhospitality, intimidation, and in this case violent heterosexual rape leading to the death of the victim. It is not about whether God's love can or cannot embrace homosexuals who share an enriching, faithful, committed love. Yet again, it has nothing to do with the issue.

Leviticus 18:22; 20:13

I shall not comment on these verses at this stage, for reasons that will become apparent later. These verses need to be dealt with so fully that they warrant a chapter of their own.

Deuteronomy and Kings

Deuteronomy 23:17–18; 1 Kings 14:24, 15:12, 22:46; 2 Kings 23:7

I shall deal with these passages together as they all refer to the same issue — that of cult prostitution. In every case, the King James Version uses the term 'sodomite' incorrectly (in the modern sense). Reliable modern versions now correctly translate the Hebrew word variously as:

- 'male temple prostitute'
- 'male prostitute at pagan worship'
- 'sacred male prostitute'
- 'male shrine prostitute'.

The treatment meted out to these cult prostitutes shows how the people of Israel felt about the sexual practices of Canaanite fertility cults. They hated them!

Because of this, and because Israel was to be a separate people, it fed back into their law.

In conclusion

This is the sum total of the relevant references in the Old Testament that is the Hebrew Bible, **and which was the Bible of Jesus, the Apostles, and the Early Church, including Paul**. The New Testament, as we know it, was not agreed as part of the canon of scripture for nearly 400 years.

We have yet to deal with the references in Leviticus (see next chapter). But apart from these there is no passage in the Hebrew Bible that in any way condemns homosexuality that expresses itself in a love which is fine and enriching to those who love one another in a faithful, committed relationship. There are only passages which condemn various kinds of same-sex sexual abuse.

Chapter 7

The Leviticus references

Leviticus 18:22; 20:13

When I first re-examined the Bible, I found that, apart from these two cases in Leviticus, the only references in the Old Testament to same-sex sexual expression were in the area of cultic prostitution and sexual abuse. So then I had to ask myself what these references in Leviticus might mean — or rather *this* reference, as the second instance simply states the penalty for the offence given in the first. Why was this written? What's it all about?

Several questions sprang to mind:

- Is this isolated reference really about the condemnation of *all* male same-sex sexual acts (i.e. the interpretation most people put upon it)?
- Or is it about heterosexual men wilfully engaging in same-sex sexual acts, when for them such acts would be an unnatural perversion?
- Or is it about male cult prostitution and other forms of abusive same-sex sexual practices as in all the other Old Testament references?

There is undoubtedly condemnation in the Bible when the act is an expression of sexual lust, exploitation or abuse. The Bible is perfectly clear on this. But does it include the expression of homosexual love for another within an enriching, loving, faithful and committed relationship?

I find it difficult to believe that it means the condemnation of *all* same-sex sexual acts, for the following three reasons:

1. It is out of character

Given that all the other references to same-sex acts are about cult prostitution or sexual abuse, **it would be the *only* reference in the whole Hebrew Bible** to include, within a blanket condemnation of all same-sex sexual acts, a true homosexual man's loving and natural expression of his love for his beloved. Yet this is just not typical of the Bible as a whole. **Where the Bible condemns, commends or exhorts, it is repetitious in its condemnation, commendation or exhortation, allowing little real room for doubt.**

Take, for example, other sexual sins such as adultery and prostitution. These are not only mentioned frequently in various forms, but are part of the fulsome spiritual imagery of 'unfaithfulness' towards the God of Israel.

Is our Biblical view of the natural sexual expression of a true homosexual within a loving, committed, faithful relationship to be based on just one Bible reference?

This is a vital question in view of the fact that the Hebrew scriptures were the Bible of the Early Church (including all who contributed to the New Testament) and for Jesus as well — a fact that will prove helpful to bear in mind when we examine two key references in the New Testament, the canon of which was not finally agreed for nearly four centuries. (In both cases Paul uses a word that refers directly to Leviticus 20:13 — see pages 43–45.)

2. Our sexuality is a 'given'
I also find it hard to accept the Leviticus reference at face value because our sexuality is a 'given' — to homosexuals as well as to heterosexuals. We are made such that we need to love at a deep level, and most of us, when we find that deep love, need to express that love physically towards the person we love within a faithful, committed relationship.

This raises an important question — one that I had to struggle with when I first reached this point in my pilgrimage. Would our Creator God have made people with a sexual attraction for another of the same sex, only then to deny the validity of its expression within a loving, committed, faithful relationship? (I didn't believe he would, but I was trying to be open to an answer either way to this question.)

3. The writers weren't talking about the same thing
There is yet a third reason I find it hard to accept the Leviticus reference as applying to sexual expression in a loving, committed relationship. When re-reading the Bible in the light of this issue, my **overriding impression** was that the writers knew nothing of homosexuality as we know and understand it today.

They wrote as though there were only heterosexual men and women, some of whom had perverted their natural desires to perform unnatural sexual acts — sometimes with others of the same sex, and sometimes with animals. Such acts either took place in the context of fertility rites, or were depraved, corrupt practices and rightly to be condemned.

Searching for further evidence

Now these three important considerations led me to believe that in all probability the Leviticus reference was either about heterosexual men wilfully engaging in same-sex sexual activity and/or about male cult prostitution and other forms of same-sex sexual abuses — just like all other Old Testament references.

But I needed further evidence in order to be more sure about this. So I decided to look at the evidence from two other angles:

- by examining any key words in the Leviticus passage with reference to parallel accounts of the same thing — in this case the Law;
- by examining the context of the Leviticus reference — the times, culture, thinking and beliefs of the people that wrote them down.

When I got to this point in my pilgrimage, I prayed hard as I studied, asking the Lord to guide me so that I would be led to his will and not dishonour him or mislead myself or others.

Comparative studies

I first explored what appeared to me to be the most likely possibility — that the Leviticus references were really to do with cultic prostitution, as is the case with nearly all the other references in the Hebrew Bible.

Now one time-honoured method for gaining further insight into a difficult text or passage is to compare different accounts of the same thing — in this case the Law. Theologians, ministers and preachers will do this, for example, when studying the Synoptic Gospels (Matthew, Mark and Luke), or when comparing parallel accounts in Kings and Chronicles.

So I compared various passages in Deuteronomy (the 'copy of the law' — see page 27) with parallel texts in Exodus and Leviticus. This proved an enlightening and interesting exercise. I found many parallels between Deuteronomy and the other two books on all sorts of matters, including one reference in each to same-sex sexual acts.

Deuteronomy 23:17 and Leviticus 18:22 are the *only* references in these respective books to same-sex sexual acts. It would seem that the law given in Deuteronomy 23:17 was parallel to that given in Leviticus 18:22. One point of particular interest is that the two texts are complementary: Deuteronomy 23:17 says that no Israelite shall be a cult prostitute, but does not specifically prohibit using the services of such — whereas Leviticus 18:22 effectively does.

The two final clues in Leviticus 18:22 and 20:13 are an often-used Hebrew word that is translated as 'abomination' [RSV] or 'disgusting act' [GNB] and the context of these verses. Three Hebrew words are translated as 'abomination':

- *sheqets*, which relates to food regulations in Leviticus 11;

- *shiqquts*, relating to unacceptable and unworthy worship of God and desecration of the Temple;
- *to'ebah*, the word translated as 'abomination' in Leviticus 18:22 and 20:13.

This third word is different from the other two. It is used of serving other gods — doing what other religions do, including fertility cult customs and practices. It is the same word that is used in connection with cultic prostitution in Deuteronomy 23:18 and 1 Kings 14:24 (as well as in over 100 other references to practices associated with idolatry).

Also, Leviticus 18:22 and 20:13 were both written in the context of passages to do with Egyptian and Canaanite religion (see Leviticus 18:3, 24–30 and 20:23, which refer to the statutes of the idolatrous cultus), thus confirming their link with cultic prostitution.

So the Leviticus references, like the others in the Old Testament, are linked with the hated Canaanite cults in which young men and women were recruited for temple prostitution. The sexual rites were supposed to 'wake up the gods' and make fertile the herds, crops and those who entered the rites. Taken together, the Levitical *and* Deuteronomical laws rightly banned any kind of involvement in these cultic sexual rites.

Practical, cultural and religious factors

There are also strong cultural reasons that point to why those Leviticus references were written, bound up with the beliefs and needs of those ancient people. Family for them was of vital practical and religious importance.

This was reflected in one of the earliest recorded commands, given in the Creation story (Genesis 1:28) to 'Be fruitful and multiply.' [RSV] The Jews learned their faith through stories (a tried-and-tested method that Jesus also used), and this particular story related to a man and a woman raising a family — a story with profound significance for their very survival.

Family was vitally important for a number of practical reasons, because large families were needed:

- to do the many chores needed to feed, clothe and generally sustain the family;
- to provide strong, healthy men to protect the tribe and to keep their women, children, cattle and crops from being stolen;
- to provide for care in later life.

In nomadic life especially, and even when the Israelites were settled in Canaan, survival depended on large families helping one another.

Family was also important because they had no concept of eternal life such as we have today in Jesus. Beyond this life there was only *sheol* — the shadowy world of the dead. So they concentrated on this life, and 'lived on' in their descendants. This was a powerful reason for the family line to continue.

It was the reason for Levirate marriage (see Deuteronomy 25:5–6), whereby a childless widow became the wife of her dead husband's brother. He would then raise up a family and thus continue the line of his dead brother. Any brother who refused to do this suffered at best a sullied reputation, and at worst death (see Deuteronomy 25:7–10 and Genesis 38:8–10).

Also, because the Jews had no concept of eternal life (as we know it in Jesus), they believed that the God of justice meted out justice in this life (see Deuteronomy 28:1–57). They therefore believed

- that God blessed the righteous with health, wealth and prosperity, security and large families (remember his promise to Abraham, who had everything else but family [Genesis 15:5–6])
- but that he cursed disobedient sinners with sickness, poverty, loss and barrenness.

It followed from this that those who prospered must have been favoured by God because of their righteousness, while the poor, sick, barren etc. must be experiencing the result of their disobedience — God was not pleased with them! We still hear people say 'What have I done to deserve this?' when things go wrong, and this is where the idea comes from.

The book of Job wrestles with exactly this problem. (It became yet another instance of where Jesus stood things on their head. In John 9:1–3, for example, the people's reaction to the man's blindness is very much according the Jewish way of thinking, whereas Jesus put a very different gloss on things.)

Large families were a joy for many reasons — not least because they were seen as a reward for righteousness. Conversely, barrenness was viewed as a consequence of sinfulness. Thus not only did women have cause to grieve when they were barren (think, for example of Rachel in Genesis and Hannah in 1 Samuel), but they also had to contend with the belief that it was their fault because it resulted from their disobedience to God. There was nothing to stop their husband taking another wife, or servant, or concubine, and fathering children in order to show it wasn't *his* righteousness that was lacking!

So strong was the need for children that women might go to extreme lengths to become pregnant. Among the best-known examples is that of Lot's widowed daughters making their father drunk and lying with him because they saw no prospect of children any other way (see Genesis 19:30–36). And in Genesis 38 the widow Tamar dressed as a prostitute and solicited her father-in-law Judah because he had not given her one of her dead husband's brothers as the law prescribed — thus she had Judah's child.

So family was vital for various practical, religious and cultural reasons. But the ancients also believed it was men that had within them the 'seed' of life (the King James Version contains many references to 'seed', such as in Genesis 21:13). Men's semen was seen as the human equivalent of the seed planted in the ground, while women in pregnancy were merely viewed as incubators. This also explains why genealogies are traced through the male line.

It followed from this that if a man deliberately 'spilled his seed' in whatever way, they viewed it as a sin against God and punishable by death (see Genesis 38:9–10). This was presumably because it took away God's prerogative to give or withhold life; it was a man's duty to use his 'seed' to raise a family.

How, then, was a man treated whose genitals had been damaged? You might expect him to be treated with compassion. Yet not only was the poor man condemned to life without a family, but according to Deuteronomy 23:1 he was excluded from the assembly of the Lord (the Temple), because they assumed he must have disobeyed God to have suffered such a misfortune.

Finally, how would they have viewed any sexual act that was clearly not procreative? They would have seen it as disobedience to God — a crime against the tribe (whose survival depended on procreation), and deliberately mocking God (who alone should decide which were the righteous who should multiply, and which the sinners who should remain barren). People who committed such acts were condemned to death for disobedience against God's command to be fruitful and multiply.

Does this still apply today?

We have just considered the most powerful cultural reason for the condemnation of same-sex sexual acts that is contained in Leviticus 18:20 and 20:13. Yet the reasons for that law in Leviticus no longer apply today! We know from our experience and from Jesus' teaching that the religious, cultural and scientific reasoning behind

Leviticus 18:22 and 20:13 was wrong. Men are not pre-eminent in having the seed of life within them. God does not withhold family because people are sinners. There is eternal life. God does not punish with death men who do not use their semen for procreation.

Nowadays, far from needing to multiply, we need restraint. It took from the creation of humanity up to 1900 AD to produce a world population of two billion; it has taken less than a century to nearly triple that number! The world is overpopulated, with people dying of starvation and disease in the very places where people still feel the need to multiply for some of the same reasons that motivated the Hebrews.

Fertility cult worship is certainly not part of the current scene. Some sexual attitudes in society pose a danger to health as well as faith. But as Christians we are aware of this and allow our faith to guide us, whether we are heterosexual or homosexual. Most importantly for this study, we know today that, just as the heterosexual act can be born of lust or of love, so the homosexual act described in Leviticus 18:22 and 20:13 can be the expression of lust, but can also be the expression of responsible, faithful, intimate and committed love. And as John explains in his first New Testament letter, where real love is, there is God. Indeed, love is God's greatest blessing — for God *is* love!

So it is *not* what we are given, but whether we use those gifts in true love, that counts with God.

We shall now move on to the New Testament references, and see if they bring us to a different conclusion when considered in context.

Chapter 8

New Testament references

The Gospels

We come to the New Testament of our Saviour Jesus Christ and what he taught about homosexuality, which was **precisely nothing!** He dealt with sexual sin. Adultery comes up in each gospel: Matthew 5:27–28; 19:9; Mark 10:11–12 (the Church sometimes changes Christ's teaching); Luke 18:20 (same as Matthew 19:9); John 4:5–42 (also John 8:1–11; see below). Prostitution comes up in Luke 7:36–50 (see below).

Christ reinforced the Ten Commandments, but interpreted the law on sexual sin, revenge etc. in a more spiritual way (see Matthew 5:27ff; 38ff), and showed great compassion for sexual offenders. Instance the woman taken in adultery (John 8:3–11): the law demanded her death, and without his protection she would have died at the hands of other sinners. Then there was the prostitute who came to Simon the Pharisee's home (Luke 7:36–50), and who is remembered as the one who, because she loved much, was forgiven much. Tradition has it that Mary Magdalen was also such a forgiven woman. Jesus did not treat them according to the law, but with compassion, even though they had committed sexual sins that demeaned themselves and others.

Did Jesus heal a sick homosexual when he healed the centurion's servant (Luke 7:2–10)? It would have been consistent with his compassionate love, and with the centurion's surprising use of the Greek *entimos* ('precious') and *pais* ('beloved servant/child/son'). Roman officers often had 'love' servants (who were dear to them) when on tour in far-away stations such as Israel. Was this servant just such a one? Roman soldiers were not otherwise known for their compassion to slaves, who were mere possessions. More usually, slaves were subject to brutal treatment and sexual abuse — that is, unless loved by their master, who then often treated them well. But perhaps this centurion was different — we shall never know.

But you will look in vain for any teaching from Jesus on the issue of homosexuality, whether positive or negative. This fact is both interesting and enlightening. The Living Word is silent, and there are only words of welcome and love. Perhaps those who take the name of Christ should behave likewise.

Paul's key letters in context

When we look at Paul's letters, there is a distinct change of emphasis and tone. Why is this?

The reason is that Paul saw the extent and influence of idolatry, and was obviously shocked by it. Fertility worship (and Emperor worship in key Roman centres) was found all around the eastern Mediterranean. It corrupted male and female, young and old alike. There seemed no limit to the depravity which idolatry opened up to the worshippers of these gods. It was believed that these fertility gods had to be 'awoken' to their work by the 'sympathetic' sexual activity of those who worshipped them — a kind of 'pump-priming'.

What had begun as worship was corroding the lives of individuals and society. **Jews had constantly to struggle to keep such worship from corrupting their worship of God. Paul saw the same problem for the Church.** The practice and influence of idolatry was especially strong in major centres of population such as Rome, Corinth and Ephesus, as well as in places like Paphos in Cyprus, where Aphrodite was said to 'come out of the sea' to influence and corrupt nations.

This is the cultural background to the three key passages in the New Testament that relate to the issue of homosexuality, which were in Paul's letters to the **Romans**, to the **Corinthians** and to Timothy at **Ephesus**.

Rome had become a moral cesspit where sadistic violence and sexual depravity went hand in hand. The Romans were by nature a cruel people. Otto Keifer describes this well in his book *Sexual life in ancient Rome*. In earlier times, the nature of Rome's religious convictions had lent disciplined strength to society. But the impact of foreign gods — the earth and fertility goddesses Cybele and Isis, and Dionysus the god of wine and happiness — brought about the decay of Roman religion, and of Roman life.

Part of the price of being a nation that had subdued others had been to become influenced by some of the nations it had subdued. The Roman writer Tacitus described Rome as 'the common sewer into which everything infamous and abominable flows like a torrent from all quarters of the world.' There were forms of 'marriage', but no constraints on sexual activity outside it. This was the norm throughout many nations in those times. And Roman festivals and initiations were a time for orgiastic pleasure — sometimes sadistic sexual activity, as some initiates were violated against their will. The mixture of sex, hedonism and violence proved a 'heady' brew.

Slavery compounded the problem. Masters and mistresses could do what they wished with their slaves, who had no rights. Lust could be, and was, satisfied with the nearest available (or most desirable) slave, with nothing to prevent it.

Rome was one of the worst centres, if not *the* worst, where all kinds of sexual abuse and depravity took place, and **idolatry and slavery** were at the centre of this corruption.

Corinth was a cosmopolitan port at the hub of major trade routes. Its character was similar to that of Rome, to whom the city owed allegiance.

Corinth was a byword for licentiousness. To behave 'like a Corinthian' meant to be debauched. Local influences such as the Temple of Aphrodite the fertility goddess, combined with a large number of people living away from their home environment, helped create a situation where 'anything goes'.

Ephesus housed the main temple of the fertility goddess Artemis — another corrupting religious influence. As the main Roman city of Anatolia, it shared all the characteristics of Rome: the arena with its games and sadistic gladiatorial fighting; its 'earth goddess' Artemis linked to Cybele, the 'goddess of love outside marriage'; as well as Emperor worship and other gods.

The corrupting effects of fertility religion were seen in many centres around the Mediterranean, but Rome, Corinth and Ephesus were among the worst, linked by trade routes and depravity. This was the scene that Paul surveyed in the eastern Mediterranean, and the young churches in those cities had to be warned. False gods and false teaching corrupted individuals and whole societies. These foul religions had the opposite effect of the gospel of Jesus, which brought *real* love and dignity to those whom the Gospel truly touched.

In the light of this cultural background, we shall now consider the three New Testament passages in detail.

Romans 1:18–32

The immorality of Rome forms the backdrop to this passage in Romans, which must be read and understood in the context of the case Paul is making for the guilt of humankind. The ancient writers of the books of Joshua, Judges, Samuel and Kings saw a pattern — a cycle — in the history of Israel, and interpreted it accordingly. In the same way, Paul saw a pattern whereby humanity goes wrong and suppresses the truth about God.

The argument begins thus (summarising verses 18–22): humankind rejects the plain truth about the Creator God, even though the evidence of his work is around for all to see. Then (summarising verses 23–25) humankind turns to idolatry, exchanging the truth of God for a lie, and the glory of God for images resembling humans or animals. (The human images were probably the statues of goddesses like Aphrodite — although Paul was probably thinking of Emperor worship too. Perhaps the most corrupting god we humans worship is ourselves. Paul would doubtless have had all these in mind.) Consequently (summarising verses 26–32) humankind no longer acknowledges God, and becomes debased in life, with passions perverted, and filled with every kind of wickedness.

So this passage is about what happens when people refuse to recognise the living God and turn to idol worship. Paul was certain of this because he had seen it. The argument hinges around verses 23–25, and also verse 26, which starts 'Because of this …' Paul saw idolatry as the reason why there was so much wickedness and depravity in the world. Worship of other gods, especially the gods of fertility, had corrupted and depraved those involved.

Rome was a major centre of such idolatry. It was not that they were irreligious but that their worship was misplaced. Every kind of sexual or other immorality was found in Rome; prostitution (male and female) and pederasty were common, and adultery rife. The situation was perhaps epitomised by Empress Agrippina, who served in a brothel out of sheer lust. People had become dissatisfied with their natural heterosexuality and its moral expression, and were turning to what were for them unnatural acts.

The picture painted by Paul, especially in verses 26–32, is not one I associate with the lesbian and gay Christian people known to me, any more than with the heterosexual Christians I know. Paul is not addressing the love of homosexual or heterosexual people — love which is God-centred, responsible, faithful, committed and enriching — but the depravity resulting from worship of other than our loving Creator God.

Those who 'tear' a verse or two out of their proper context here to condemn *all* homosexuals and *all* same-sex relationships — including the truly loving expression of that sexuality — are, sadly, abusing the scriptures.

In Romans 8:30–34, Paul writes:

> '… those whom he called, he also justified … If God is for us, who can be against us? … Who will bring any charge against God's elect? It is God who justifies! Who is to condemn? It is Christ Jesus, who died, yes, who was raised, who is at the

right hand of God, who indeed intercedes for us.' [NRSV]

And as we are reminded in Romans 8:1:

'There is no condemnation for those who are in Christ Jesus!' [NRSV]

1 Corinthians 5:9–13; 6:7–11
Corinth was like Rome in its sexual immorality. Sexual immorality (a man sleeping with his stepmother) had raised its ugly head in the church, so Paul was worried and angry (1 Corinthians 5:1, 9–13). In 1 Corinthians 6:7–9 he inveighs against various wrongdoers as he develops the point he is making: that by going to law against fellow Christians they are no better than the wrongdoers he goes on to list in verses 9–10.

But take careful note of the people to whom Paul is referring. For this is quite different from the logical argument he sets out in Romans. It is a list of the wrongdoers who, he believes, will not inherit the Kingdom of God.

In describing the sexual sins, Paul uses four Greek words; the first two are:

- ***pornoi*** — the sexually immoral (Paul has already used this of the man sleeping with his stepmother);
- ***moichoi*** — adulterers.

But it is the other two words that are often used to condemn homosexuals, so let's look more closely at them:

- ***malakoi*** means literally 'soft', and in the sexual sense it seems to refer to the passive partner in male prostitution; it is equivalent to the term used in Deuteronomy 23:17 (see page 30), which is how it is translated in the NIV and NRSV:
  - — 'male prostitutes' [NIV/NRSV]
  - — 'homosexual perverts' [GNB]
  - — 'sexual perverts' [RSV]
  - — 'catamites' (boys kept for same-sex sexual acts) [JB].
- ***arsenokoitai*** derives directly from those texts in Leviticus that we examined in chapter 7; Paul is pointedly referring back to Leviticus 20:13, where the phrase *ho an koimethe meta* ***arsenos koiten*** *gunaikos* ('he who lies with a man as with a woman') would have been familiar to him from the Septuagint (the 3rd century BC Greek translation of the Hebrew Bible).

The Leviticus reference, which we have already examined in context in chapter 7, is almost certainly where Paul gets his word from. This word, which is extremely rare, is used only twice in the New Testament — both times in Paul's letters. In view of what Paul saw on his travels, he may well have used the term to include other forms of sexual abuse between males such as prostitution or pederasty, where lust and not love was the motive. But we don't know. We simply know the origin of the term, and that Paul, a former Pharisee and Rabbi steeped in knowledge of the Law, would have known that too.

When we look at the interpretation of *arsenokoitai* in modern versions of 1 Corinthians 6:9, we understand the difficulty the translators must have had. They come up with:

— 'homosexual perverts' [GNB]
— 'sexual perverts' [RSV]
— 'sodomites' [NIV/JB/NRSV].

These translations generally seem to be reflecting the corrupt morality of Corinth rather than the origin and associated meaning of the Greek term. And of course, by the very nature of things, there were bound to be many more heterosexual perverts than homosexual perverts!

Before we go on, just a brief comment on the GNB's use of the term 'homosexual perverts' for both *arsenokoitai* and *malakoi*. The word 'perversion' means literally 'wrong or bad use' of something — in this case sexuality. Of the various translations, the RSV probably comes closest to the spirit of the Greek, though the activities described would no doubt have included mostly *heterosexual* perverts. But let us consider the GNB's translation 'homosexual perverts'. Any heterosexual would agree that 'heterosexual perverts' refers to those heterosexuals who pervert their sexuality, and that this *doesn't* imply that all heterosexuals are perverted. Well, the same applies to the term 'homosexual perverts'.

The same-sex sexual acts that Paul writes about in Corinth all involve abuse and perversion. They may be committed by homosexuals, heterosexuals or both. They are acts which undermine the worth and dignity of those involved. But again, this does not fit the case of responsible, loving, faithful gay and lesbian Christians. Like some heterosexuals, there are some homosexuals who damage themselves and others with their lusts, abuses and perversions. Equally, there are many responsible homosexual people, as there are heterosexual people, in loving, faithful, committed unions blessed by God.

But this is something which Paul did not touch on. He seemed unaware of it, just as he seemed unaware of other things that we are aware of today. So again, we find that a general condemnation, especially of faithful homosexual Christians, is misplaced.

After 1 Corinthians 6:9–10, Paul goes on to write in verse 11:

> '... and this is what some of you used to be. But you were washed, you were sanctified, you were

> justified in the name of the Lord Jesus Christ and the Spirit of our God.' [NRSV]

This is the gift to all who are in Christ — and as the man said in Romans 8:1:

> 'There is no condemnation for those who are in Christ Jesus!' [NRSV]

1 Timothy 1:3–11

We have already noted that Ephesus housed the Temple of Artemis, the fertility goddess (see Acts 19:21–28). The artefacts made by the Ephesian craftsmen depicted a many-breasted woman, sometimes with two stags — a significant symbol!

Ephesus was also the main Roman city of Anatolia (Asia Minor), subject to all the various Roman influences. Like Corinth it was on a major trade route and therefore subject to the influences brought in by travellers. Much the same can be said of Ephesus as of Rome and Corinth. There were the same violent games, the same gods, and the same licentiousness and depravity.

It was here that Timothy was stationed when Paul wrote to him from Rome. In 1 Timothy 1:3–5, Paul writes about false teachers — those who

> 'occupy themselves with myths and endless genealogies ... rather than the divine training ... which aims for love that comes from a pure heart, a good conscience, and sincere faith.' [NRSV]

He goes on in verses 9–10 to list those who are 'lawless and disobedient, godless and sinful, unholy and profane ...'

Later on this list he includes the words *pornois* and *arsenokoitais* — forms of two Greek terms that we have already seen in 1 Corinthians — although this time, interestingly, he does not include *malakoi*. How do the principal Bible versions translate these terms?

- ***pornois***
  — 'immoral' [RSV/GNB]
  — 'immoral with women' [JB]
  — 'fornicators' [NRSV]
  — 'adulterers' [NIV]

This term is again translated in terms of heterosexual sin, and the NIV opts for a very restricted meaning.

- ***arsenokoitais***
  — 'sexual perverts' [GNB]
  — 'perverts' [NIV]
  — 'sodomites' [RSV/NRSV]
  — 'immoral with boys and men'[JB]

Again, bearing in mind the Levitical origin of *arsenokoitais*, the translators seem to interpret it in terms of what was known to be going on at Ephesus. In essence this is about male prostitution and other forms of same-sex sexual abuse associated with idolatry and false religious teaching.

This is in stark contrast to what Paul said in verse 5:

> '… love that comes from a pure heart, a good conscience, and sincere faith.' [NRSV]

Now this sounds much more like my gay and lesbian Christian friends. I certainly don't recognise them in Paul's description in verses 9–10.

Paul's other letters

Paul wrote many other letters to churches, including those of Galatia, Ephesus, Colossae and Thessalonica, and there are some common themes running through all of them. One of these is sexual immorality, which is rife everywhere. All his letters contain strong words about this.

We have to remember that in the ancient world, sexual relationships outside marriage were normal and accepted. Sexual appetite was something simply to be gratified. It was Christianity that brought morality into this aspect of life.

But note that Paul does not use the terms *malakoi* or *arsenokoitai* again.

Galatians 5:16–21

Paul was concerned that people should know real love and not its counterfeit, which in verse 19 he describes as:

- *porneia* — 'sexual immorality'
- *akatharsia* — 'impurity'
- *aselgeia* — 'debauchery'.

Take a look at what the modern translations give in verses 19–21, and then compare this with verses 22–23:

> '… the spirit produces love, joy, peace, patience, kindness, goodness, faithfulness, humility and self-control. There is no law against such things as these.' [GNB]

It is such a spirit that I find in my lesbian and gay Christian friends.

Ephesians 5:3–5

Just before this passage, Paul has been comparing the old life with the new, calling on his readers to live in love and renounce the old ways. In verses 3–5 he describes the sexual sins of those who will not share in God's Kingdom as

- *porneia* — 'sexual immorality'
- *akatharsia* — 'impurity'.

Take a look at how some modern versions translate these verses. Then think about lesbian/gay Christians and their experience of Christ in relation to Ephesians 3:20–21:

> 'To him who by means of his power working in us is able to do so much more than we can ever ask for or even think of …' [GNB]

This passage raises an obvious question. Given that Paul sent this letter to

Ephesus, which is where Timothy was when Paul wrote to him (see page 45), why does he not include *arsenokoitai* here as he does in 1 Timothy?

The reason this letter does not contain this same specific reference to same-sex sexual abuse is because it was not written for the Ephesians alone, but was a circular letter to all the churches (see Colossians 4:16). Whenever Paul wrote specifically to a church where he knew people, he included greetings to them. Now he knew and loved the people at Ephesus, but there are no greetings in this letter because it is not specific to Ephesus. That he did not use the term *arsenokoitai* either is another indication that it is not specific to Ephesus.

Colossians 3:5–9

Again, Paul is contrasting the old life with the new. In verse 5 he tells his readers to put to death the following things:

- *porneian* — 'sexual immorality'
- *akatharsian* — 'impurity'
- *pathos* — 'passionate desire'.

Take a look at how some modern versions translate these terms.

In verse 11 Paul goes on to write of those who are in Christ:

> '... there is no longer Greek and Jew ... Christ is all and in all.' [NRSV]

Likewise, in Christ there is no longer heterosexual and homosexual; Christ is all and in all.

1 Thessalonians 4:3–7

In this passage Paul describes the sexual sins that God wants us to be free of:

- *porneias* — 'sexual immorality' (v.3)
- *pathei epithumias* — 'lustful desire' (v.5)
- *akatharsia* — 'impurity' (v.7).

Again, look for yourself at how some modern versions translate these.

In the passage leading up to this, Paul comments (1 Thessalonians 3:12–13) that in Christian love (*agape*) and holiness we are blameless before God. In his letters, Paul is constantly contrasting Christian love (*agape*) with various Greek terms which amount to counterfeit love. He can see temptations and dangers all around, especially for people who have previously been involved in such things, and he rightly warns them.

He is particularly worried when someone is tempted and overcome, as in Corinth (see 1 Corinthians 5:1), so that for a moment, in his anger, he feels the only way is to remove the offender — throw him out of the church.

Later on, as Paul remembers his past life and how he was forgiven, so he entreats them to restore the offender.

To sum up

In his letters Paul was attacking sexual immorality generally. But in his letters to **Rome** and **Corinth**, and to **Timothy** at Ephesus, he mentions a form of sexual immorality that was a particular problem in those cities:

- When writing to the Roman Christians, he includes a graphic description of the same-sex sexual abuse and depravity springing from idolatry.
- When writing to the Christians at Corinth and to Timothy at Ephesus, he uses the terms *malakoi* and *arsenokoitai* to convey what he has so graphically described when writing to the Romans.

But neither of the two terms occurs in any of Paul's letters apart from these two — to the church at Corinth and to Timothy — which is another reason why *arsenokoitai* (a word based directly on Leviticus 20:13) should not be seen as a word of general condemnation. Otherwise Paul would have undoubtedly used it in other letters.

Given the context of the situation that Paul's converts faced, his letters and language are understandably strong on the subject of sexual immorality and abuse of all kinds, including male same-sex prostitution and abuses like pederasty. But nowhere at all does he even write about, let alone condemn, people who are in loving, faithful same-sex relationships.

When he writes specifically about same-sex sexual activity, it is always in the context of idolatry, lust and sexual abuse — never of the enriching love that can be shared by homosexual Christian partners in a truly loving relationship as enjoyed and shared by any married man and woman.

So Paul's writings cannot be used to condemn such love. It would be blasphemy to condemn it, for such love is born of God — it is the very essence of God. When people do condemn, they do so in ignorance, both of Paul's writings and of the love they themselves condemn.

Some final instances

Revelation 21:8; 22:15

In two passages in the last book of the New Testament canon, John writes about those people who will be kept outside the gates of the city — the New Jerusalem that has the 'tree of life'.

Among the groups mentioned in both instances are the by now familiar *pornoi* — the 'sexually immoral'. But there are no graphic descriptions of same-sex sexual abuse such as we found in Romans 1, nor does he use the term *arsenokoitai*.

In the second passage John does use the term *dunes* — literally 'dogs' — which some people incorrectly link with homosexuals. But it is actually used to refer to male prostitutes (see Deuteronomy 23:18 [KJV]), and sometimes even to false teachers (see Philippians 3:2 [GNB]).

To conclude

So there we have it! Nowhere does the Bible condemn truly loving expression, whether sexual or otherwise, between homosexuals in a relationship that is loving, committed and faithful, because the biblical writers seem to know nothing about such people or such relationships.

As with other gifts, it is not what we are given, but what we do with those gifts, that the Bible applauds or condemns.

We may use our sexuality to love and enrich another, or we may use it to debase and destroy the dignity of others and ourselves. It is the use to which we put our gift of sexuality that concerns our God and his word.

The Bible condemns sexual immorality and abuse of all kinds — hetero-sexual and homosexual. But it encourages true love, whether love for God, or *agape* love for others, or friendship love, or enriching, faithful sexual love for a beloved. All such love — true love — is given by God. It is one of God's greatest blessings.

God has made a world full of rich variety in every way. If we care to see it in this way, we can praise God for its richness. It is only when, in our ignorance, we refuse to acknowledge things as they are — wanting creation to be in a nice tidy order that we can understand — that prejudice blights the lives of good people who are different from us.

> 'Whoever lives in love lives in God and God in them' [NIV]

These words from 1 John 4:16 are profound truth, and apply to homosexual people just as they apply to heterosexual people! God has a purpose for all his people, including his gay and lesbian people — consider what Paul says in 1 Corinthians 1:26–31.

The homosexual Christians I know hold to God's purpose, they are faithful in Christ, and God gives them the power to love others with a love that is righteous and acceptable to God in Jesus. That is enough for God; it should be enough for God's people — the Church.

Chapter 9
Gay Christians and the Church

There are some amazing stories in the New Testament about the early church and the Apostles. There is the remarkable conversion of Saul — a Rabbi and an important Pharisee, taught by Gamaliel himself — a Jew of the Jews, with utmost respect for the Law and separation from the Gentiles. He was to become Paul, the apostle *to* the Gentiles. You will no doubt be very familiar with his story.

In Acts 10 we find a story that is no less amazing. It is about a man called Peter — a fisherman, a pillar of the Church. He, like Paul, was fastidious in keeping the Law. As regards the Gentiles, he didn't eat with them, he wouldn't go into their homes, and he would only associate with them when absolutely necessary. That was the Law, and that was how he played it.

Then he had this vision about unclean foods:

> 'Rise, Peter. Kill and eat!'
>
> 'Not so Lord. I have never eaten anything common or unclean.'

Three times the voice challenged:

> 'What God has cleansed, call not that unclean.' [RSV]

Peter responded amazingly well when he understood what God was saying to him. For it was new truth — difficult new truth. Such truth was to throw to the wind many of the things he considered precious and holy.

But not only did he go to Gentiles to proclaim the gospel; those Gentiles were the hated Roman conquerors. His obedience opened the gate for the Gentile Pentecost!

Yet there is a sadness in what I have to say here. For Peter saw no further than the immediate challenge. It was a big challenge, but he interpreted it only in the sense of what he was called immediately to do. It was a staggering new truth, the breadth of which he did not seem to appreciate fully.

And not only Peter but the Church has interpreted that vision in too narrow a sense. The Church continually has to learn afresh the lesson of Peter's vision. A big struggle is needed to persuade the Church to appreciate how broad the interpretation of this vision could and should be!

The struggle for women in the ministry still going on, 2,000 years after this magnificent vision that speaks to us. Traditionalists are still fighting the battle against that great truth.

And the struggle goes on to persuade Christians to welcome homosexual people — men and women — into the full fellowship and ministry of the Church. We are still not listening to that voice which says:

> 'What God has cleansed, call not that unclean.'

I have come to the conclusion that much of the intolerance in the Church — and it is not universal, thank God — is due to ignorance about the sexuality we call 'homosexuality', and lack of experience of meeting homosexual people while being aware of their sexuality.

This is one of the reasons my wife Carol and I arranged occasional get-togethers over a buffet meal, for homosexual Christian friends from the Essex LGCM Group and heterosexual Christian friends, people who have previously been to a Bible study and discussion group where the issue has been properly addressed.

It takes some courage for homosexual Christians to 'come out' to people they have not previously met, as well as for those who meet them. People come apprehensively, but the ice is soon broken, and they go away saying how good it was to meet each other and have the opportunity to talk.

We all know homosexual people because there are so many of them. But so often we just don't *know* we know them! If we did, many of the false images we had of them would evaporate. We would find we are just like each other! We would find that they fill many of the posts in our churches, at all levels. They are to be found in all walks of life. There would be so many astonished people if homosexuals, especially those who are Christians, all declared themselves.

The sad thing is that many homosexual people have been hurt so often that they cannot trust us with their truth. This is our problem, and we need to address it. All that most of us know of lesbians and gay men is when one of them fails and we see it in the TV and newspaper headlines.

The good news is that lesbian and gay Christians have so much to offer the Church. Apart from being loving, faithful people, they include many very gifted people among their number.

And they have much to teach us of Christ, who was himself despised and rejected. We need to think how we can work together for the Kingdom of God.

We need each other

From what I have learned, one of the problems homosexual people, especially Christians, struggle with when they enter a loving relationship is the lack of role models. There is no knowledge of homosexuality as we understand it today in the Bible, so there is neither specific guidance nor a 'role model' for those who live in a committed, loving, faithful relationship with a partner of the same sex. The only guidance that the Church offers at present is nearly all negative.

There are of course some general guidelines, such as faithfulness, love and commitment in relationships — values that enrich our most important relationships, and give them stability.

And Christian scholars like Jeffrey John are working at developing role models. His book *Permanent, Faithful, Stable* says a good deal about the direction this is taking.

Obviously there is a problem about children: homosexual people are denied so much, and I know for some this a great loss. It is easy for those of us who don't understand to say that they should therefore get married. But pressures on marriage have never been so great, and to add the pressures of a homosexual wife or husband is to place any marriage under almost intolerable strain. While some survive, almost inevitably many such marriages fail. There is so much for us to think about here — so much to understand. Much compassion needed. Such issues represent the difficult side of the equation.

But there is another side of the equation too — the fact that homosexual Christians are as faithful as, if not more faithful than, most heterosexual Christians.

They have had to struggle with their faith as few other Christians have, and to work through that barrier of tension that has traditionally equated homosexuality with evil. But they know the Lord has called them, though many of them are mystified and mortified at his people's response to them.

I know their love is genuine Christian love, and I know they need to be affirmed — not only to be accepted but to be loved with Christian love. And as Carol and I know from experience, this love is something which will be returned with good measure.

We have shared worship and fellowship with lesbian and gay Christians for a few years now. We have found great understanding for those who have hurt them. And never has there been anything said or any suggestion made that made us feel uncomfortable, or question whether we are doing the right thing. Rather, have they gone out of their way to welcome us, despite our representing those who cause them problems. We are shown love and respect, even though in our ignorance we have doubtless sometimes said things that have caused some pain or hurt.

Our experience leads us to hold a high opinion of them as Christian people — as faithful, God-loving, Bible-respecting Christians. But they are not to be intimidated. They know who they are. They know they cannot change that part of them that has caused them such problems. In faith they have come to terms with it and know that they are a precious part of God's Kingdom people.

They are not going to go away — or rather I hope they are not going to go away! We need them for without them we are incomplete.

We in the Church are called by Christ to love them, and part of loving is seeking to understand. We should welcome them as Christians into every part of the Church. We should work with them to provide a basis and proper recognition of their 'covenant' relationships. If we do not do these things, we will have failed to obey the command of Christ to 'love one another as I have loved you.'

A few years ago Carol and I were invited to join a weekend conference of Christian fellowship and worship with some 30 lesbian and gay evangelical Christian people. It was a time of Christian love, healing and joy. I gave to them as I opened the scriptures that are in this book, and affirmed them in the love of God. Carol and I received as we shared with them in all the things they had planned — prayer times, worship and sacraments, meals, and of course, conversation and laughter.

Just before that conference, Carol and I had been through emotional turmoil on account of an experience that had befallen one of our family. I was left with deep anger inside. That anger was healed as the agape love of our friends there surrounded us. I was renewed by the love of Christ within them.

Isn't this how it's meant to be? Loving, sharing, supporting one another in the love of Christ.

Bibliography

Reference books

During the writing of this book I have gained enormous assistance from a large number of reference books, but the following have proved particularly helpful:

- *Peake's Commentary on the Bible* ed. by M. Black & H. H. Rowley (rev. ed., Routledge, 1991) ISBN 0 415 01547 9
- *Dictionary of the Bible* by J. Hastings (T. & T. Clark, 1909) o.o.p.
- *Religious ideas of the Old Testament* by H. Wheeler Robinson (Duckworth, 1913) o.o.p.
- *Young's Analytical Concordance* ed. by R. Young (Lutterworth Press, rev. ed., 1939) ISBN 0 7188 0021 4
- *International Critical Commentary* series (T. & T. Clark)

  — *Romans* by Sanday & Headlam (rev. ed.) ISBN 0 567 05026 2

  — *1 Corinthians* by Robertson & Plummer (rev. ed.) ISBN 0 567 05027 0
- *Groundwork of Biblical Studies* by W. D. Stacey (Epworth, 1979) ISBN 0 7162 0293 X
- *Sexual life in Ancient Rome* by O. Keifer (rev. ed., Constable, 1995) ISBN 0 09 474480 7
- *Living in Sin?* by J. S. Spong (Harper Collins, 1988) ISBN 0 06 067505 5
- *Permanent, Faithful, Stable* by Jeffrey John (Affirming Catholicism, 1993) ISBN 0 232 52075 5
- *Cambridge Greek and English New Testament* ed. by J. Scholefield (Parker) o.o.p.
- *Daily Study Bible* series (St Andrew Press)

  — *Romans* by W. Barclay (rev. ed., 1975) ISBN 0 7152 0277 4

  — *1 Corinthians* by W. Barclay (rev. ed., 1975) ISBN 0 7152 0278 2

Versions of the Bible

The following versions of the Holy Bible have been used; as most are available in a variety of editions, only the imprimaturs are given for each:

- **Revised Standard Version**
  — Division of Christian Education of the National Council of Churches of Christ in the United States of America
  — British & Foreign Bible Society
- **New Revised Standard Version**
  — Division of Christian Education of the National Council of Churches of Christ in the United States of America
- **Good News Bible**
  — American Bible Society
  — The Bible Societies
- **New International Version**
  — International Bible Society
- **Jerusalem Bible**
  — ✠ John Cardinal Heenan (on behalf of the Roman Catholic Church)
- **King James Version/Authorised Version**
  — crown copyright